SOME CURSORY REMARKS

SOME CURSORY REMARKS

MADE BY JAMES BIRKET
IN HIS VOYAGE TO NORTH AMERICA
1750-1751

 BOOKS FOR LIBRARIES PRESS
FREEPORT, NEW YORK

First Published 1916
Reprinted 1971

INTERNATIONAL STANDARD BOOK NUMBER:
0-8369-5682-6

LIBRARY OF CONGRESS CATALOG CARD NUMBER:
77-150169

PRINTED IN THE UNITED STATES OF AMERICA

PREFACE

The diary here printed under its original title, "Some Cursory Remarks made by James Birket," came undoubtedly from the collection of Dr. William Thornton, now on deposit in the Library of Congress. It was preserved by Mrs. Margaret Bayard Smith, the wife of Samuel Harrison Smith, founder and first editor of the *National Intelligencer,* and descended to Mrs. Smith's grandson, J. Henley Smith.

Of Birket himself nothing is known, beyond what is stated in his itinerary. He was probably one of Thornton's West India friends, a merchant and sea-captain living in Antigua, where the name is found among the records sufficiently often to establish the presence of a Birket family there. Among the Thornton papers is a little brochure, *The Ladies' Advocate, a Poem,* printed in Antigua in 1748, which bears the name of James Birket, the owner. How the diary came into Thornton's hands we do not know. Presumably it was given to him by Birket, either in Antigua or in Tortola of the Virgin Isles, where Thornton lived, and must have contained information which the latter would value, preparatory to visiting the United States, as he did some years later, when he took up his residence there.

PREFACE

It is evident from the diary that Birket was in more or less frequent communication with many of the merchants of the Northern Colonies, and probably acted as correspondent and factor for them in their commercial dealings with Antigua. His observations show the mercantile bent of his mind and contain information that is not easy to obtain elsewhere.

C. M. A.

SOME CURSORY REMARKS MADE BY
JAMES BIRKET

SOME CURSORY REMARKS

MADE BY JAMES BIRKET
IN HIS VOYAGE TO NORTH AMERICA

1750

July 26th at two O'Clock P.M. sailed from St. John's Harbour in the Island of Antigua, in the Ship Knowles George Sibley Commander for Portsmouth on Piscataway river in New Hampshire, Henry Rust a young man of that Place and myself Passengers, this and the Two following days seasick and had as smart a breeze a Cross the trade as I ever met with 　　　　　　　　　　　　　1750

This day crossed the Tropick nothing remarkable; Fresh gale, 　　　　　　1750 July 29th

This evening it begun to blow & we had a violent gale of wind at S.W. Lat. 32° 34′ about 10 o'Clock at night Sprung our Missin mast across by the deck 　　　Augt 4th

This morning the Strength of the gale being somewhat abated about 7 oClock (the sea runing high) I observed a flock of Gray Plover which came close by the Ship and Seamd to fly directly to the So Et we being then in the Lato of Bermudas and abt 2° to the westward of it, which confirmd me of the Truth of 　　5th

[1]

SOME CURSORY REMARKS

the Ano^r here, that these birds come from N. America to the West india Islands in July & Augt yearly, where they stay a Small time And then leave them to Seek fresh commons elsewhere

7th   This day the weather being a little cool, I drank some beer to my dinn^e not having drank any before Since 17 Ap^e 1747

1750
Augt 11th   This 3 or 4 days past fine weather and this day caug^t a Sherk 10½ foot long and by Computation see Above twenty Grampuses standing to the S^oW

12th   We caught some Mackrall and see a sword fish along side of the Ship about eight foot Long Exclusive of the sword of Snout that seem^d to be above 3 foot long which was the only one I ever saw

13th   We took near ½ bble of Mackrall wth in Georges bank from 9 @ 16½ Inch Long

14th   At 3 P.M. made the land called Egamenticus which are blue hills that lye 30′ or 40′ fro: the Sea, we see also to the Eastward near as far as Casco bay

15th   This morning at one A.M. made the Isles of Shoals which are sundry Small Islands about 2 leagues from the mouth of Piscataway river upon the largest of which are 50 or 60 familys which make a Small town in which is a Presbyterian Meeting house & A minister that resides Amongst 'em

Augt 15th
1750   their chiefe subsistance is by fishing as the Islands is an Entire bed of rocks which produces no herbage or Any kind of Corn, grain, or Timber we were becalm^d near those Islands & Standing of and on all this day which furnished us with a fine Prospect

[2]

MADE BY JAMES BIRKET

not only of these Islands but the main land also, which we were very near this afternoon and Expected to have been put on Shore by the Eddy tide in Shore but Escaped and put of to Sea again

Calm all the forenoon Several people came in a boat to us where we lay, from the Isles of Shoals and about 12 o'Clock came from Portsm⁰ in a boat Capt Mills, Paul Marsh & 2 Others, Soon after they came on board we observed the Breese come towards us, At one P.M had a fine breese and got round fort Point at New Castle at 3 oClock & at 4 got up to the wharfe at the town of Portsmouth where came on board us
Mark Hunting Wentworth Esq
Jotham Odiovne Esq
Cole⁰ Messerve
Capt Nathl Pearce
Mr. High Sherriff, Packer
Capt Ryon, Capt Burt & Sundry others at 7 oClock after regailing our guests we came ashore and Spent the Evening at the Widdaw Slatons with Paul Marsh Captain Pearce & Several others— where I lodged and intend to do So during my Stay in this place being the best tavern for Strangers in town

 I Dined with Mark H^s Wentworth
 D⁰ with Wm Keating at Capt Wm Pearsons
 D⁰ with Capt Nat. Pearce at Geo Jeffrys
 D⁰ With Jotham Odiovne
 D⁰ with John Sherburne
 D⁰ with George Libby
 D⁰ with Henry Sherburne Esqr

16

Augt 16
1750

17th
18.
19
20.
21.
22
23

[3]

SOME CURSORY REMARKS

Augt 24 1750- Went with Henry Sherburne in his Chair to Exeter 15 miles fine road & dined with Coleo Gilman; this town is Scituate upon a branch of Piscataway river, where they have a large Wooden bridge over the Same where there is severall saw mills Grist mills &Ca and here the build Ships of good Burthen, this– Branch of the river being Navigable up to the town which is well built and Pleasantly Scituated there is two Presbyterian meeting houses here, one of the Newlight And one of the old, but 'tis hard to Say which Sees best there Seems to be 100 houses or more in the town, some of them built after the modern taste which make avery good Apearance; The People here as well as in Other branches of Piscataway river complain that there Lumber is far to fetch out of the Country and Stand, them very dear, which realy seems to be the case

1750 for the road that we went was extreamly well Inhabited all the way and the ground generally Cleared and as far as we could see beyond the town, but indeed one cannot see far here as the country is so much upon alevel that it's few Places that Afford any distant prospect, Abundance of Lumber is brought down to this town by Land carriage and afterwards is rafted down the river to Portsmo in the Evening we returnd with Geo Libby and Henry Rust in Compa

25th Dined with Jotham Odiovne
26 Dined wth My landlady Slaton
27 Do with Do – And this day captain Sams from Bidiford agreed wth M H Wentworth & Coleo

MADE BY JAMES BIRKET

Miserve to build him a double deck vessel About 100ton for which he is to pay them in goods at 1100 pCt and to Allow them £30 pton The Exctra: is now reckond at 1000 pCt there first agreemt was to take the goods at 1200 pCt but the Gentlemen Aledged there had been an Advance put upon the goods and therefore Insisted on the above Abatemt The goods were chiefly courseCloths and aKind of duffilds like ordinary bearskins, Camblets, Shallons, Plushes, and Some All spuns, Ironpots,– Pewter, Cordage, Course rugs & Blankets, Allsort of shipnails, Shoes & Boots course Hats, Ready made Cloaths, and other kind of coursegoods
 Another Captain from the same Place agreed for aSmaller vessel at 25£: pton and topay in goods 25 pCt on the Sterlg Invoice, but this vessel, being ⅔ finishd as aSale vessel, was deem'd avery indifferent one both as to wood and workmanship as that sort generally are

Augt 27 1750

  dined with my Landlady Slaton   28th
  Do at Capt Pearsons with Wm Keeting   29th
  Do with my landlady Slaton   30
  Paul Marsh Edmd Quncey Junr and Ctpt Newmarsh and myself got aboat And went up the river as far as Quochecho, aBranch of Piscataway river about 12 Mile above Portsmo where we went on board a Sloop loaded with Lumber that was brought down to to her from Quochecho Town The Country along this river on both Sides is very full of Inhabitants There we See aSix vaind wind mill and those well Supply'd with the Necessarys of life

31th

Augt 31 1750

[5]

SOME CURSORY REMARKS

About Dover we observed the land much freer from Stones and more of aSandy Soil, never the less we see many large Orchards Loaden with fruite and Abundance of Maze in their fields; got home in good time and dined wth Landlady Slaton

I shall now attempt aShort discription of New Hampshire and the town of Portsmouth &C^a Just as it Occur'd to me during my Short stay there, as I intend to Set out towards Boston Tomorrow Morning,

Augt 31 1750

The river of Piscataway– being the only one of any note within this Province, and I think exceeds any I have yet seen, for the extent of it, And lyes about WNW: & ESE 'tis said to be from 7 @ 16 fathom at low water with aBold Shore and has many creeks & Coves where there is good Anchorage out of the tides way for the largest ships, it is of aModerate breadth from ¼ to ½ a mile, and at some points that Jetts out into the Stream Still Narrower, Again in other places above the Town it extend, itself to a great Breadth; From the Fort point at Newcastle where it disembogues itself into the sea to the Town of Portsm^o Commonly caled by the Country People (Strawberry bank) is three miles, and the extent of its Navigation is in Some branches 12 in others 18 or 20 Miles for Small vessels, as to Exeter, Dover, Berwick and Quochecho And other places where they have Saw Mills, Grist mills, &C^a but for their larger vessels they bring their Lumber down in Rafts to the bank where the said vessels lye to take it in

MADE BY JAMES BIRKET

Formerly this river was well stored with Salmon which they took in plenty but of Late they have quite forsaken this river, Occasion'd as its' believed from the Number of Sawmills on the different branches of P. river, the weirs of which runing crop the same And the Sawdust from the pine, which its believed is very ungratefull to the fish when Mixed with the Water and has Occasion^d them to Seek for fresh quarters, The river below the town and for some miles above the Same is well Stored wth Codfish, Bass and several other Sorts of Choice fish, Lobsters they bake in abundance near their wharfs

This river makes a very grand & Genteel apearance at the Enterance for for On the Larboard hand going from the Sea you have the Antient town of Newcastle with a fort upon the point, And in the town a large Meeting house with avery high Wooden Spire Steeple which you See many miles at Sea, As you Also do another tall Spire of the Same Sort on the Starboard hand going in Called Kittery, where is the Seat of that great Command^e Sr William Peperill Generall of the Army that Re-duced Cape Briton And the City of Louisburgh after a Long and Close Siege; there is also Several other handsome, neat houses Near Sr Williams, as his Sons and also his soninlaw Sparrowhawks, both which make a good apearance from the river

N.B. this river divides the province of New Hampshire from the province of Main to the Eastward which last is in the Massachusets bay & all the other countys to the Eastw^d

SOME CURSORY REMARKS

The Town of Portsmouth is Scituated upon Piscataway river about 3 miles from the sea upon aModerate rising ground, not only from the river, but also from the Adjacent country to the Parade or Center thereof; where 4 Principal streets meet in the nature of a + there are pretty Streight and regular through which you have a prospect of the country on every side; the other Streets are Irregular. &Crocked with many vacant lots not yet built upon, and most of em now made use of in gardens &C^a as the town Stands partly upon a point that Jetts out into the river it makes very good Conveniencys for Building wharfs and warehouses on each side out of the Strean where Ships of any Burthen may lay & discharge their cargos into the warehouses wth out Expence or trouble

The houses that are of Modern Architecture are large & Exeeding neat this Sort is generally 3 Story high & well Sashed and Glazed with the best glass the rooms are well plasterd and many Wainscoted or hung with painted paper from England the outside Clapboarded very neatly and are very warm and Comodious houses one thing I observed there that they lay all there floors double, not Crossing each Other but that the seam or Joint of the uper course Shall fall upon the middle of the lower plank which prevents the air from coming thro' the floor in winter or the water falling down in Summer when they wash their houses

As to their Publick Buildings the have aChurch of the Establish^d religion for church of England

MADE BY JAMES BIRKET

(which is the only one in this Governm^t) they have also two Meeting houses for the Presbyterian or Independent perswasion All three built of wood with tall spires to each which you See a long way off at sea, indeed all the houses in town Save two are built of wood Their Court house has been formerly adwelling house and is now aScandalous old building ready to tumble down; they have no other buildings worthy of Notice —— The better sort of People here live very well and Genteel, They have no fixt market but the Country people come to town as it suits them with such of the Commoditys as they have for Sale by which the town is pretty well Supply'd with Beefe, Mutton, veal, and other Butchers Meat; they have plenty of large Hoggs and very fat bacon, they have also abundance of good fish of diferent Kinds, And abundance of Garden Culture as Beans, Peas, Carrots, Parsnips, Turnips, Radishes, Onions, Cabages Colliflowers, Asparagus, English or whats commonly called Irish Potatoes also the Sweet Potatoe, Obtains almost alover North America, More so to southward, They have also Apples Pears, Plumbs, Cherries, & Peaches in a Abundance They have also Apricots & Nectrines from England, but do not Observe they had given any of them the Advantage of awall, there's likewise Gooseberrys Currant D⁰ Rasberries, Strawberries, Huckleberries Water & Muskmellions, Squashes and Sundry Other kinds of fruits roots &c &c There common drink is Cyder which they have in great Plenty, and New England rum And also new

SOME CURSORY REMARKS

rum from the Westindies, But People of fortune (especially the Marsh's) have very good rum and Madeira wine in their homes, Indeed the wine most commonly Drunk here is from the Canaries &Western Islands— called Oidonia, tis of a pale coll^r tasts harsh and is inclined to look thick

There taverns are very Indifferent & little frequented by any but Strangers

This town enjoys afine Air by Standing upon arising ground and comman^d a fine prospect from the Center every way and is Certainly the most agreeably Scituated for Pleasure or Bussiness of most places I have Seen

This Government or Province of New Hampshire is bounded to the Northeast by Piscataway river wch Separates it from the Province of main, &Countys of york & Cornwall, And to The S.W. by aline run to the N E of Merrimac river about 2 miles which devides it from the Massachusetts bay 'Tis about 18 miles wide but the length from NW. to S. E. I could not learn; The ground in this Country is mostly alight Soil, Inclined to be Sandy, &some places more of a Gritty and Gravely nature and not capable of bearing Much dry weather, yet being not often broke up is very Productive in Seasonable years, they raise Oats &Barley but their Chiefe grain is Maize or Indian Corn of which they plant a good deal but not Enough for their own Consumption being Obliged to Import large Qu^{tys} from Maryland &Virginia, Also from New York &Philadelphia from the 2 last places

MADE BY JAMES BIRKET

they have all their flour as their own Country will not produce any wheat, They have Abundance of Large Orchards And Make great Qtys of Cyder wch is their Ordinary drink, they also export a good deal to Hallifax, Terre Nova N&S. Carolina &C, This province also produces Good Hops &Exceeding good flax of which the Irish Settled at London derry Make very good Cloth & fine Ounce thread, Some of the Cloth I see which was choise good Shirting Linnen and I am informed this little town increases very much, This Province abounds with rocks and large Stones but they are of such a Stubborn nature and break so Crossly that they are not fit for any thing except field fences & not good even for that; The land seems Capable of grain more than Sufficient for their Own Consumpt but the people up the the rivers Seem more eager after Manufacturing the Lumber, And those below y^t are near the Sea, Are either Seamen Fishermen &C^a So that between the two the land Seems to be a good deal Neglected, Tho'it Seems generally capable of Cultivation as it's near upon a levell wth Small risings and fallings, Sufficient to cary of the water after rain but you have not any hills of any Considerable height for many miles the nearest you See is reckoned 40 or 50 miles from you in the inland part of the Country, yet the ground in general is dry and very good roads for road horses or Carriages

The Exports of this province are Chiefly Lumber, as Boards, Plank, Joists, Staves, Shingles &C which come mostly down the River from the differ-

SOME CURSORY REMARKS

ent Branch^s also fish which the Send as well as the Lumber to the West Indies and the latter also to the Straights &C^a they have also Sent a good deal of Lumber to the City of Hallifax and Nova Scotia & Terre Nova &C^a Altho they complain that it is very dear to them the Cartage out of the woods to the mills being now a long way and the wood dear to what it used to be Their present Price Curr^t Seems to be for Boards Plank & Joists 16 @ £18 pms, Ship building ½ goods ½ Cash 25. @ 30£ pton Rum 28@33 pGall Masts 16 Inch 75 feet Long £20, Clapboards 16£ pms Shingles £ pms Extra a London 900 pC^t or 10 for 1

As to their woods, they are of different Kinds their Oak is esteem'd — the best timber in the Northern Collonies for Ship building of which they carry on a very great stroke which they send to the Westindies and Europe and there dispose of them, they have also— Several sorts of pine some much more Serviceable then Others which they Saw into boards plan & Joists Some that are cut Down and Shipt to England for Masts for the royal Navy, there is also great q^tys of masts cut and Lumber made to the E.w^d as far as Casco bay where large— Ships loads Masts for the Kings y^ds And abundance of Lumber is here Shipt in Small Sloops for Boston they have also Ash, Beeach, Wallnut of sundry Sorts very large Chesnuts And Sundry other Kinds of wood

I do not find there is any Iron works in this Province for in the last year they paid a Most Intolera-

[12]

MADE BY JAMES BIRKET

ble price for Iron which they Chiefly have from Maryland Virginia & Pensilvania, Not only for Shipwork but all other uses

Their Cattle are small but Seemingly very strong having Short thick bodies and Short Limbs, Their Horses are also Small but very Hardy & Strong their Sheep are Small but the meat very Sweet fat & well tasted they have plenty of Poultry as Geese Turkeys, dunghill fowles Ducks &C^a tame; And plenty of Wild Turkeys in the woods also Wild geese & Ducks Partridge much Smaller than ours Also abundance of small birds as Blackbirds who have a note much like frogs in a Summer Evening they Keep in prodigeous flocks; the have also, a Bird like our field fare with a red Brest which the call a Robin that sings delightfully, I also See the Humming bird here in the Month of August——

This day about 11 o'Clock left Portsm^o with man Yorkshire on two hired horses in Comp^a with Capt Wm Pearson & William Keeting who Set us on our way about 6 miles, We got to Hampton to dinner being 9 miles, In the afternoon we View^d this town as we rode along being pleasantly Scituated in a fine open country, on the west side of which is a large tract of middow Ground where we see as we passed them abundance of Stacks of salt hay cut in these Middows, They let the Stacks remain until the frost come And enable them to fetch it home at Other times the ground is too soft & bogy to go upon with any Kind of Carriage being frequently overflow^d by the tides especially near the river From Hamp-

1751
Septeme 1st

SOME CURSORY REMARKS

1751
Sepr 1st

ton to Newburry is 11 Miles where I arrivd about Sun Set And then found myself near two miles in Boston Government we Crossed the river in a Sailing ferry boat and landed in Newburry, At my landing met with Capt Woodbridge who went with me to a tavern or Inn Kept by one Ebenezr Chout where we had a pint of wine &C This river that washes the borders of Newburry is called Merrimack & is about a Mile in Breadth at the town and of a prodigeous extent back into the Country as may be Seen by the maps, Tis of a good depth at the town for Shiping but they are obliged if large, to waite for Spring tides to Come in as there is a Bar at the mouth of it that has not above 10 feet at Low water but is above 16 feet at Spring tides. It is not Navigable much above the town being full of rocks & Shoals Notwithstanding the bring down great Qtys of timber for Ship building which the turn into ye river above the falls, And the Stream brings it down as it does also Staves & Shingles made Up in Bundles which are also turn'd into the river and so pickt out again by people that attend on purpose about the town and deliverd to the Owners thereof

This river is the most remarkable for Salmon of any in those parts and now more so as they have forsaken Piscataqua as before Observed

Newbury is a pretty good town Scituated on the Wt Side of the above sd river in the Collony of the Massachusetts bay, And Extends itself near a mile on the bank of the river, with two long Streets which

MADE BY JAMES BIRKET

run Paralell wth the river and Several Cross Streets It is pretty well Built, And has 2 large presbyterian Meeting houses And one Episcopal Church, but that is without a Minister Consequently the Sheep are Scattered. Here is carried on a Great trade in Ship building, I reckoned 26 upon the Stocks in the town besides w^t was Launch^d and then in the river And what was building in Other Parts Adjacent, I lodged at Ebenezer Chouts——

Being first day, I rode about two miles into the Country to a Meeting at Haveril dined at a friends house Close by & return'd to Chouts in the Evening   Sepe 2d

This morning set out for Ipswich being 11 Miles, got there in two hours being Excellent road I baited here, This is a pretty large Inland Town Scituated upon a fine river but not Navigable so high as the Town There is a Large Presbyterian Meeting h^o in the Middle of the Town, the houses here seem to be mostly old And upon the decline they have Some Coasting vessels that come to below the town at at some distance where they discharge and take in their Loadings reCross^d this river at the end of the Town by a Wooden bridge, from This Town to Beverley Ferry is 10 miles and one on the other Side to Salem, This last stage is most Excellent Road, even, Smooth and hard Gravell——   Sepr 3d

I dined at the widdow Pratts at Salem and Spent the afternoon with Capt Ingersoll & Capt Pointon who are my Old Acquaintance, Lodged wth Capt Ingersoll, Salem is a large Town well built, many genteel large houses (which tho' of wood) are all

[15]

SOME CURSORY REMARKS

*plasterd on the outside in Imitation of Hewn Stone, Here is a good Harbour for Small vessels, and Several good Wharfs & Warehouses & a good trade to the Westindies for their fish and Lumber &C.

About 4 miles from hence S^{o}Ward Stands the town of Marblehead, I was not there as it lyes Something out of the road to Boston and the way to it is very Stoney & Rugged they carry on a good trade in fishing having not less then 160 or 170 Sail of Scooners intirely Imploy^d in that Branch of Bussiness And A merch^t there whose name is Hooper— Sends up the Straights 5 or 6 vessels of his own with fish every year

Sepr 4th   This morning Set out for Boston with Capt Pointon's Mare & Chair & left one of my hired horses at Salem from which the 1st Stage is to Linn being 8 Miles this is a Neat Pleasant Country Town or village but very Irregular from Linn to winisimet ferry, or Chelsey ferrey is 7 Miles, and from thence over the Bay to Boston is Reckoned One & A Half mile

And I am of Opinon tis near two miles I drove the Mare and Chair in 2½ hours from Salem to the ferry which is 15 Miles at Least; we got over the ferry by Eleven o'Clock And dined at a Widdow Womans Near the ferry, and after dinner went to the Exchange Tavern & from thence to Capt Hugh Canes & took Lodgings at one Arthurs for myself and Man Yorkshire

* This is a Mistake they are pland & Painted

MADE BY JAMES BIRKET

Nothing remarkable this day dined at My Lodgings   Sepr 5th

Dined with Capt Hugh Cane & after dinner took a Walk with him & Wm Husbands round the town to See what was most Remarkable   6th

Dined with Jacob Ryall Esqr in Comp^a with Henry Vassels & in the Evening went with said Vassels to Cambridge in his Chase being 8 miles the land way but Over Charles town ferry tis Only Recon'd 4 Miles——   7

Return^d from Cambridge to Boston In Henry Vassels's Chase by way of Charles Town where we Crossed the ferry and dined with Capt Combes Charles Town is pretty Large & a Country town Scituate upon a Peninsula between Mistick river & Charles River & is Caled the Mother of Boston being Settled before it & parted from Boston only by Charles River over which there is a ferry very well Attended & the River here is as broad as the Thames at London, This town has two large Streets that Come down towards the ferry, and Handsome large Meeting House & Good Market place It has but Little trade as Boston is so Near it most people in trade Choose to live there   1750 Sepr 8th

Being first day dined at my Lodgings being much out of Order with the Cholick & A Cold in the Evening went home wth H Vassels to Cambridge in his Chariot——   9th 1750

Henry Vassels & Self went in his Chace to Dorchester to dine with Col^o Robt Oliver being 9 Miles   Sepr 10th

SOME CURSORY REMARKS

Returned in the Evening; This is a very Pleasant country town And Stands about 4 Miles from Boston, here the Land Seems to Exceed any that I have Seen in this Country, & their Orchards Seem to be of the Best fruit trees And are very large which enables them to make abundance of Cyder; Old Parson Jn⁰ Chickly & his wife came from Providence In a Chair 47 Miles & Lodged that night with Henry Vassels

Sepr 11th We went with a Couple of Country Clergymen, Conducted by Hancock one of the Tutors to See the College at Cambridge, Which Consists of three Separat Brick buildings which was Errected at different times The first About the year 1638 and called Harvard College from one Harvard who was a

1750
Sepr 11n great Encourager of it, And as their Stock Increased they added two Other Large buildings, One of which is called Stoughton hall, And although the 2 wings do not Join to the Middle builds yet they are So placed As to form a very handsom Area or Courtyard in the Middle, there is also a Small Chapell where the Students hear prayers twice every day they are About 100 in Number, and as likely well looking young men from about 15 to 20 years of age as any I have Seen, They have a Large & Commodious Library but the books are mostly Old And not kept in that Order One could wish, They have also Some Natural Curiositys but in no regularity nor do they know what many of 'em Are——

1750
Sepr 11 The Town of Cambridge is well Scituated On Charles River which is Navigable to the Town and

MADE BY JAMES BIRKET

over wch there is a very good wooden bridge but has no trade (being too Near to Boston) the Inhabitants depends Chiefly on their Courts &C. being the Chiefe of a County And the Colledge &C There are Some good homes here and the town is laid out very Regular, but for want of trade One 4th part of it is not built The Country here abouts is well Cleard and the ground looks very Promising for Corn or Grass After our return from the Colledg dined with H Vassels———

H. Vassels, One Ellerey, Old Chickley And myself Went in 2 Chases to Castle William, which Stands upon an Island in the Bay 3 Miles below Boston and 12 from Cambridge where we dined with the Captain Chaplain &c in the Great Hall— This fortification was built very early after the Settlement was made, but very Irregular, upon which King William Sent over An Engineer to repair the Same, Instead of which he demolished it, And Errected a more regular Fortress in its room and Called it Castle William, Since wch Com^o Knowles has added greatly to its Strength by an Additional Battery, which mounts a great many Guns, So that now it may be reckon'd Amongst the Strongest fortifications in Our America A regular Watch being Kept night And day, And not a vessel passes into Boston Harbour, or out w^thout being hail'd from the fort,–as the only Good Channel for Shiping lyes Close Along the Shore of this Island and within Pistol Shot of the Castle Where I believe there is not less then 150 pieces of Cannon a great Q^ty of

Sepr 12

*1750
Sepr 12th*

SOME CURSORY REMARKS

Small arms, And a Considerable Number of men always upon duty

1750 Sepr 12th About 2 good leagues below the fort or Castle Stands a very good lighth° for the Direction of Shiping, and in war time the make Signals to the Castle upon Seeing Any number of Shiping by Lowering & hoisting a flag as many times as the See vessels in the offing

13th Return^d to Cambridge in the evening H. Vassels Brought me down to Charles Town ferry in his Chase & then return^d I came over and dined wth Capt Cane But was invited to dine with Isaac Ryall Esq upon his Commenceing a C   of the Horse 'twas Said he that day Entertain^d between 3 & 400 men, And Supos^d it lost him a Couple of Thousand Pounds O T——

14th I dined with Capt James Forbes & Spent the Evening With Capt Jno Lang from Whitley who was building a Ship here for the Coal trade——

15th I dined with Foster Hutchinson & Spent the Evening wth James Griffin One of their Most Eminent Merch^{ts} And an Agreeable man

1750 Sepr 16 Being the first day of the week I was At Meeting and dined with my friend Benj^a Bagnall Sen^e And in the Evening took leave of Boston And Went in the Charrot with my friend H. Vassels to Cambridge and Also Man Yorkshire & our baggage

BOSTON is a large well built town (& by some writirs Called a City) Chiefly of Brick altho there are a good many Wooden houses that make a very

[20]

MADE BY JAMES BIRKET

good figure, 'Tis Computed to be near two miles in Length from Charles Town ferry, to Fortification Gate upon the Neck And Six in Circumferrence And to Contain About 3000 houses And 20000 Inhabitants; the Streets are all well paved a thing rare in New England, And in the North End of the town Crooked, Narrow, And disagreeable but from the State house S⁰ward fine Open Capacious Streight Streets from the Gov^er House to the Stateh⁰ is one of the finest I saw in america Called Cornhill, Also King street which Extends from the Statehouse to the head of the Long wharf is A curious fine Open Genteel Street At the uper end of which, Near the end of the Statehouse (which the walk in, in Bad weather) the Merchants meet every day about Eleven o'Clock & Continue continue until near One before the retire to dinner: Amongst whom you will find very good entertainment, And their houses furnished in an Elegant manner Their dress very genteel & In my Opinion both men & Women are too Expensive in that respect

1750
Sepr 16

There Publick buildings are, first the State or Province house where the Governour his Councele and the Assembly, or house of Representatives meet to make laws &C^a And a large Room for the Courts of Justice to be held in And the ground room as before is made use of as a Charge at times— Fannivelle Hall, built by Peter Faniuelle & cost as it is r^d £20000, which he gave to the Town the botton part for a Market house & Above Stairs for the Transacting of Publick affairs of the Town

SOME CURSORY REMARKS

1750
Sepr 16

But what is Surprizing to Strangers before it was Accepted b the town It was put to the vote whether or no it Should be Accepted of and was Only Carried by 6 or 8 votes So great is the Aversion of the vulgar to any Publick or Stated markets, or Market days which is now in Some measure got the better of, There is Nineteen different places of Worship in the Town (to wit) thirteen of the Independents Presbyterians & newlights &C^a but I look upon the Church of Boston to Consist Chiefly of the first, two Baptists Meetings three of the Established Church of England which Seems to me to gain Ground all over New England, Also One Quaker Meeting h^o So Called, by the Map of this town the Author Makes 17 Spires Cupola's &C^a Two of which I find to be his own Invention & Imposition on the Publick; this town Stands upon a Peninsula which is Joined at the South End by A Narrow neck of Land in Some places not more then 40 y^{ds} broad,

1750
Sepr 16

(and pallisado^d Across, with a Strong gate to Pass through when they go out, or come into town) And at the bottom of a large bay guarded from the Sea by many fine Island, Several of wch are inhabited & have Excellent Pasturage, this harbour is large & Comodious for Trade having a Sufficient depth of water which allows the vessels to come up to the wharfs one of which *called the Long wharfe is near half a Mile in Length running from the Bottom

---

*This is the Boston people's Acco^t But Since have been Informed by one who Measured it & found it to be only 700 y^{ds} in Length See the Conclusion of this Itinerary

[22]

MADE BY JAMES BIRKET

of King Street directly into the Harbour, where vessels lye moor'd to it in great Safty and discharge there Cargos into Warehouses that are Errected upon the Northside of S^d Wharfe almost the length of it, besides this there are vast Numbers of other wharfs Warehouses & Docks &C where vessels Load & Discharge there cargos wthout the help of Boats Lighters &C and Great ease to the People

The trade of Boston Seems to be upon the decline in my Opinion, for I do not see Any thing they can call a Staple amongst them Save Ship Building and Somthing of the fishing trade, and that cannot be called properly their's, as it is not taken by the Inhabitants of Boston but those of Cape Ann, Marblehead, & Salem, where they go to purchase their fish for Exporta^n and their Oil &C from the people of Nantucket, Their Lumber from the Gov^t of Piscataway, york County, the Province of Main, & as far to the Eastw^d as Casco bay, There are the Chiefe Articles they export, as to Imports they have a good Share, viz large q^{tys} of Dry goods of all Kinds, from England, Rum, Sugar, & Melassas from the West indies, & Bread & flour from Philadelphia, also Bar Iron for which they Send them Rum of their Own distillation Some refin^d Sugar, & Some fish &C^a And the rest in cash whilst they had it, but now there is little of that left Since they have by an Act of Assembly called in all the Province bills & Issued out of the Treasury the Dollars (to the Amo. of £170,000 Sterg̃. and upwards) granted

1750
Sepr 16

1750
Sepr 16

SOME CURSORY REMARKS

them by Parliment towards defraying their Expences in going agst Cape briton as they were very much Straightened to make their Remittances Especially to England these dollars has been almost every one of em Picked up for that End so that at present they seem to be without money or Credit, which is a Miserable Scituation

They are esteem^d to build the best Ships here in any part of North America, for the goodness of work & their wood is not Inferiour, if they Choose the best, but there is So many Sorts of Oak here, that a Stranger is in great danger to be Imposed upon except he meet with a faith full man and Such are not always to be met wth by Strangers; The Artificers in this Place Exceed Any upon ye Continent And are here also Most Numerous as Cabinet Makers, Chace & Coach Makers, Shoe Makers, Taylors Peruke Makers Watchmakers, Printers, Smiths, &C &C The Merchants are Numerous but many of them want bottom to Carry on An Advantageous & Extensive trade Others of 'em tho' not many, have Acquired Opulent fortunes and with great Reputation

there has been Built here in one year (i.e. in the Province) 700 Sail of vessels 200 of which were from 100 to 200 Ton And 1000 Sail has been Clear'd out of this port in One year, but now their woods are very much Cut down and destroy'd and what they have is brought along way by land Carriage in many places, which makes building Come much dearer than formerly

1750
Sepr 16

MADE BY JAMES BIRKET

Continued at Cambridge boug^t a horse from One Stedman for £160 OT. And hired Another for Yorkshire

Set out for Rhode Island, H. Vassels And his Wife, Mary Phips The Lieu^t Gov^{es} Daughter wth Two Servants &C To Accompany me So far on my Journey, Our first Stage was 19 Miles to A house Kept by one Robins where we dined upon Roast^d Partridges Fat bacon & Irish Potatoes now plentifully Produced in that Part of the world & tollerably good, In the Afternoon we travelled 19 Miles more to One Mother Stacks, who I thought realy very Slack in her Attendance for twas with great Intreaty and fair words that we obtained a Candle altho twas So dark when we lighted that we could Scarce See Another & What was worse She had nothing in the world for Supper However upon Rummaging the Chace box we found in our own Store a Couple of Roasted Fowles Some white biscuit, Lemons, Rum, Sugar &C So that out of our own Store we made out a Handsome Supper & Liquor to it but could not do So well for Lodgings our Beds being very Indifferent——

This Morning we passed Sea Conk plain being about 3 miles over wthout a Shrub and quite Levell, Sorround^d with woods makes no disagreeable apearance, here we left Providence road upon our Right hand and proceeded to one Hunts at Rehoboth being 9 Miles where we Breakfasted, from thence we Came through Some fine tall woods of Oak timber the best I had yet seen to Swansey ferry being 4

Sepr 17th

Doo 18th

1750
Sepr 18th

Sepr 19th

SOME CURSORY REMARKS

Miles which we passed in very heavy rain, And Came to Bristol before dinner, Dined at One Widdow Pains a Private house but sent Our horses to the Tavern

Bristol is a Small town but regularly laid out in Squares many lots in which are not built One large Desenting Meeting h^o besides which I did not See any Other Publick building

This Town lyes at the bottom of Rhode Island bay or harbour has good depth of water,–And Several Wharfs where a vessel may lye And there Load & Discharge at Pleasure; But the Town of Newport seems to draw away Most of the Trade from this as Most Large places do from new Settlements Notwithstanding they have Some vessels in the westindia trade and build many vessels here And in the Neighbourhood—— It is a proverb here that Bristol is Only remarkable for its plenty of women and Geese

Sepr 19th 1750   After dinner we went to Bristol ferry being 2 Miles and Crossed the Same where we Entered upon the N.E. End of Rhode Island and Came the Same Evening to New Port being 12 Miles and Lodged at the late Deputy Governour Wm Ellereys but Sent our horses to the Tavern

Sepr 20th   We all dined with Our fr'd Ellereys Lady he being out of Town and in the afternoon I left my Comp^n there and went to Capt Jno Jepson's where I lodged as Also my man & horse during my Stay in R. I,

Sepr 21st   I dined with Capt Jonathan Thurston

MADE BY JAMES BIRKET

I dined at John Jepsons and in the Afternoon I went with my fellow travelers to See Captain Molbons Country house It Stands upon a tolerable Advantageous Scituation About a mile out of the Town And makes a good Appearance at a distance, but when you came to Survay it nearer it does not Answer your Expectation It is Built of Hewn Stone and all the Corners and Sides of the windows are all painted to represent Marble, You Enter from a large flight of Steps into the first Story which is very Grand the Rooms being to Appearance 16 or 17 foot high but the upper Story is Neither of the proportionable in the height of the rooms nor Size of the Windows the Cellars Kitchins &C are below Stairs 'tho Only upon the Surface of the Earth before the house is a Handsome Garden with variety of wall fruits And flowers &C; this house & Garden is reckond the wonder of that part of the Country not being Such another in this Government

22d

Sepr 22d 1750

N: B we Enter'd this Governm^t of Rhode Island at Bristol ferry wch Parts it from the Massachusetts-bay

This day I was 'twice at Meeting which is very large; the Meet^g house is also large and has two tier of Gallerys And a Cupola on the top, but the friends in my Opinion are as Topping as their house, for I did not Imagine one half of the Congregation had been of that Society and I afterwards found they were not to be known by their Language dress, or behaviour Altho' there Seems to be a few w^n (Compair'd with the whole) that are very Exam-

Sepr 23d 1750

SOME CURSORY REMARKS

plary in every respect and an honour to their profession and the Society; this day dined wth my landlord Jepson——

24th This Morning I Accompany'd my good friends Henry Vassals & his Spouse And Mary Phips on their return back as far as—Bristol ferry which is 12 Miles where I took leave of 'em & return^d to J^no Jepsons to dinner

25th I dined wth Capt John Thurstone
26. I dined wth our fr'd John Easton
27. I dined wth Capt J^no Brown Merch^t
Sepr 28th I dined at Jonathan Thurstons
1750
29. I dined at Abram Redwoods
30 I dined at J^no Jepsons & was a Meeting
Oct^e 1st I dined with D^o
2d I dined with Joseph Whipple this day we walked over the hill behind the town to the Beach and to Nich^s Eastons where we See his little dear park and his pond where he keeps his wild geese, brants, & wild ducks &C^a

Newport is the only town in the Island and Stands on the NW Side thereof and Near the West end, and upon arising ground from the Sea or harbour is in the General well built And all of wood (Except the Statehouse and one of Capt Molbons which are of Brick) the houses in general make a good Apearance and also as well furnished as in Most places you will meet with, many of the rooms being hung with printed Canvas and paper &C which looks very neat Others are well wainscoted and painted as in other places The main Street is called a Mile long

MADE BY JAMES BIRKET

and runs Paralell with the Harbour besides which there are Several other Streets and lanes which are regular and pretty well built, That part of the town called the point is also laid out in Squares and pretty well built, they have abundance of good wharves which Extend the whole length of the town where vessels of any burthen can Load, discharge, or heave down without the help of Lighters which renders it an Excellent Scituation for trade and more Especially as it is so near the Sea that vessels are out or in, in a Moment, notwithstandg the labour under one great inconvenience that is their Ships & vessels are subject to the worm and more particularly at the point where the best water is but this is only in the Sum^r time

They have one Wharf which by way of preeminence is Called the Long wharf and runs from the bottom of a Spacious wide Street (at the uper End of which Stands the Statehouse fronting to the Sea) about half a Mile into the harbour And then turns with an Angle and Joins it Self to the point, There is a Number of warehouses built upon this Noble wharf in Imitation of that in Boston and in one thing Exceeds it by the Joining to the Mainland at both ends it forms a fine Bason Where Small vessels lye very safe in the Winter time Entering by the Drawbridge that's placed about the Middle of the said long wharfe

1750
Oct^e 2d

There is Several publick buildings in this Town worthy of Notice, viz' the Statehouse which (as before) Stands at the upper end of a Spacious wide

SOME CURSORY REMARKS

1750
Octo 2d

Street fronting to the harbour, is built of Brick and is a Genteel Large buildg There is a large meeting house for the friends as before Observed; One with a large handsome Steeple for the Presbyterians; one Do for Do Somthing Smaller One for the Church of England which is very neat and Genteel, and pretty large; One of the 7th day & one of the first day Baptists, there is also a good many Jews but the have no Sinagogue, They have here a very Handsome Library built upon the hill above the Town and is well adapted for the use designed being Only one Story but the floor raised Several Steps, and from thence they have a good prospect of the Harbour And Neighbouring Country Abram Redwood Made a present to the Said Library of £500 Sterg. value in books on Sundry Subjects.

Here is abundance of Transient French Merchts which are concerned with the people in trade to Cape Briton, Cape Francois, &C. They have also a good trade from hence to the Coast of Guinea, The Bay of Honduras for Log wood which the send chiefly to Holland and have alsorts of dutch goods in return which are all run by the Connivance of good natured officers who have a feeling Sence of their Neighbours Industry, They have also a good Trade to the wt India Islands with flour, Pork, Shingles, Staves, Boards, Horses, &C the Chief of which the Purchass from their Neighbours in Connecticut Governmt

1750
Octoe 2d

This Island is throughout like a Garden from the Industry of their farmers who keep there ground

MADE BY JAMES BIRKET

very Clean Their fences are Chiefly of Stone made by themselves to Save their wood a piece of Industry rarely met with in North America, They do not grow any wheat, but Some Oats and a good deal of Maze & they have Excellent grass and fine Cattle, the largest by much I see in America

Their Curr'y which is Chiefly Paper is Esteem^d upon the worst footing of any in N. America and depreciates in value every year, yet the Legislature are Generally ready to Issue a fresh bank, upon the Aplication of Any one of their Learn'd body who frequently make good use of those Opportunitys

I set out for New York in Comp^a with my worthy friend Geo: Mifflin this day about 10 o'Clock I hired a horse for Yorkshire from Capt Jos^h Scott who is now Sherriff

Octoe 3d

We took boat at the Point & in about 2 hours landed upon the Island of Connanicut being 3 Miles but the wind blowed very Strong agst us, we then Crossed this Island beg one Mile to the Next ferry but it blow^d So hard we could not get over So was Obliged to dine with an ill natured Scold at the ferry house who gave us Potatoes & Tatogue with an intolerable dirty Cloth &C however after the Dinner we got over the ferry being 3 miles, in Two hours the wind Continuing to blow hard agst us, from hence we had 5 Miles to one Caseys at Tower hill very bad Stony Road, this is reckon'd one of the best houses of Entertainment in the Governm^t but being Court time & a number of People there we

Octoe 3d
1750

[31]

SOME CURSORY REMARKS

did not Stop, but proceeded Along the Naraganset Country 9 miles to Sq^e Hills at Charles Town where we Lodged, This Country is very Subj^t to Stones &C And uneven——

Octoe 4th 1750   We were up early this morning in order to Proceed on our Journey w^n Behold our horses had made their Escape out of the Stable and being late before they were found, & yorkshire who went in Pursuit of 'em with Hills Indian Boy did not return till after Sunset Obliged us to Stay here another night in the Meantime my Fellow Traveller & Self, went out a Shooting Kill^d some Squirrels and some very pretty birds called Marsh quails Something bigger then a field fare and fine Eatg we also went to See the Pallace of the King of the Narraganset Indians but he being a Minor & With his Grandmother about 9 or 10 Miles up the Country at another Town, we were deprived of a Sight of his Majesty, Our Landlord Hill told us that he has got a good many Subjects that are Sober Religeous People and about 20,000 Acres of land in his Own right which he &

Octoe 4th 1750   his Ancestors have held theirs even since the discovery of this Country by the English and no doubt long before Some Gentlemen in Newport are a kind of Guardians to him and receive his rents, Lease out his lands &C^a for him during his Minority as well to the Whites as his Own Subjects

Octoo 5   We Set out pretty early after riding a mile We left the Indian Wigwams on Our Left And their Kings palace on our right which is but an Indifferent

MADE BY JAMES BIRKET

house Built of Stone two Story high, the Glass very much broke and Otherwise to Appearance very much out of Repair, we travelled through a great deal of Stony uneven road until we got to one Cole⁰ Williams who keeps a house of Entertainm^t So Called at Stoninton being 21 Miles where we dined upon Salt pork and Turneps with thick Cyder to drink, here we Cross^d Mistick river at a wooden bridge, and So proceeded through Groton a very Stoney uneven Country but no high land only full of Small hills or risings & fallings 9 Miles which broug^t us upon the banks of the river Thames Opposite to New London we Crossed this river by the ferry boat where it is esteem^d a mile over & took up our Lodgings at one Capt Bradocks formerly a Sea Captain who behaves with great Politeness & Good Manners to his Guests when Compared with the rude lazy drones of this Part of the world 1750 Octo 5th

We took a Walk about a Mile out of town to See Capt Thos Olliver at his house, The Surface of the ground is almost Cover^d with large immovable Stones that makes it mighty difficult to Plough &C here; they Sow Some wheat & Rye, Oats &C^a Abound in Orchards And Great Plenty of Fruit and Make Abundance of Cyder Spent the Evening with Mathew Stewart who treated us very kindly And in a very Genteel manner Octoe 6th

We walked to Capt Olivers and dined with him, his Neighbour Capt Duffy & An Other Gentleman dined there also Octoe 7 1750

NEW LONDON is the Capital of the County of

SOME CURSORY REMARKS

that name And pleasantly Scituated upon the river Thames ab^t 5 miles from the Sea (or more properly the Sound that lyes between long Isl^d And the Continent) And is Navigable for vessels that draw *20 foot water there is but few vessels belonging to this port which are Chiefly in the west india trade, But as it is one of the Chiefe ports in Connecticut Governm^t Many vessels that are Owned in Other parts of the Governm^t come here to Clear out and go under the Name of New Londonery, They have Some very good wharfs here wch their vessels lay along Side of to load or discharge; The town Seems to Improve by the Appearance of their houses many of which Appear New And Neat all built of wood & Consists of one Street about A mile long by the riverside, Altho' upon the Bank which is of a Moderate height and as Several lots on that Side the Street are not built it affords a fine prospect over the river and the Adjaient Country; There is in this Town One Episcopal Church and One Presbyterian Meeting house and now we are Enter'd Connecticut Government, The Chiefe of the trade of this Place Consists of Lumber, Porke, Horses &C to the westindies

1750
Octoe 7th

Octoe 8th
I bought a little mare from One Silas Cooke a Shoemaker to Mount Yorkshire upon which cost me wth Saddle & bridle £89 OT– and Left J: Scotts hired horse to be return^d by the post, and we Set out with our fr'd Capt Thos Oliver who proposed to See us on our way as far as New Haven We had very Stoney road to the rope ferry which is 6 miles we got

* or any vessels w^tever

MADE BY JAMES BIRKET

over very well being So narrow that a rope is Stretch^d aCross for the Safty of travelers as the tide runs here with great violence, from hence to Say brook ferry is 12 Miles which is Near half a Mile wide and Crosses the Great River Called Connecticut which runs through the heart of this Province and is Navigable about 60 Miles up the Country as far as Hartford the Capital of the County & has a Considerable trade inland there is also two other towns that Stands on Each side the Conflux of this great river called Saybrook & Lime which have not much trade from Saybrook ferry to the widdow Lays is 7 miles Baited from thence to Killingworth 5 miles where we Lodged at one Merrils a very poor Indifferent house & had lodgings had Roasted Oisters for Supper Killingsworth is a pretty long Village of one Street of Houses The Land here abouts appear^d to me to be rich and good and by Industry I believe wo^d produce plentifully

Octoe 8
1750

From Killingsworth to wst Guilford is 20 Miles, Breakfasted at one Johnsons West Guilford is a large Country town with two Meeting houses of the Presbyterian Perswasion one, of the New and the Other of the Old light and a Church And a large Spacious green in the Centre of the Town and a fine Country about it, but no Navigable river; From hence to Branford is 10 Miles dined at one Proctors this is a Small Country town from hence to NEW HAVEN is 10 Miles 3 miles from which we crossed a Small ferry and a mile from that nearer Newhaven

Octoe 9th
1750

SOME CURSORY REMARKS

Octoe 9th
1750

we Cross a pretty river by a Long wooden Bridge where the tide flows above it considerably here we joyn the upper Road from Boston that runs through the Country at a Considerable distance from the Sea & comes through Hartford, Wallingford &C^a here the produce wheat, Rye, Hops & abundance of Maze or Great corn which they Ship of at Newhaven where we Arriv^d this Evening and Lodged at one McNeals an Irishman who keeps a tollerable good house Compared with what you meet with in common

NEW HAVEN is the Capital of the county, And covers a great deal of ground And has been laid out Regularly, but only built upon here and there it looks very indifferently, It is a Seaport & was Settled very early and was then the Capital of the Province, it is well Scituated for Trade being near the Center of the Government, Here the Councele & Assembly Sit in this Month, here is also the County Goal And two large Presbyterian meeting houses one of the Old the other of the new light, Likewise a Colledge for the Education of youth Called YALE COLLEDGE, it is built of wood And Consists of one Long Narrow fabrick with Brick Chimneys running up the back part of it at Convenient distances the whole seems to be very much decayed, (which has put them upon building A new one of Brick which Seems to be About 3 foot Above the Ground & And will front towards a large Spacious green in the Middle of the town, there is in this Colledge a Very pretty Library And

MADE BY JAMES BIRKET

well kept, their Books are many of 'em of Much Later date and better Choose then those at Cambridge They are Obliged for a good part of them to the late Dean Berkley now Byshop of Cloyne in Ireland, they have also Some Curositys in this Library And Some Aparatus for Natural & Experimental Philosophy This town has more Advantages then Any other in this Governm^t as being A seaport, a great deal of Publick Bussiness transacted here as Courts & the Sitting of the Councell & Assembly And the great highroad that runs through North America and which divides about two Miles to the Eastw^d as Mention^d Above As Also the Colledge which Brings many People here from different parts of the Country Especially at the Commencem^t The Ground about this Town is exceeding levell and produces well but is not reckon'd So rich as it is farther up the Country——

Octoe 9 1750

This Morning Set out for Milford which is 12 Miles, (the Residence of Gov^{e}Laws) but the place being very Sickly did not Stop in it, It is a good large Country– town but no Seaport, we Kept on to Stratford ferry which is 4 Miles further which we Crossed and then turn^d out of the road 2 Miles to See Sam^{l}Lyons at one John Pimms where he lodg^d found him Exceed^g weak, we dined there & then Return^d to Stratford 3 miles it Rain'd Excessive hard both the forenoon and this afternoon we Called at A house here but could not have Entertainm^t So we rode on to Pembroke farm, being 3 miles And

Octoe 10th 1750

SOME CURSORY REMARKS

Octoe 11th

Lodged with one Lewis there who keeps a decent Clean house
We Set forw^d this Morning & breakfasted at Fairfield at one Penfields & had Chocolate & Plenty of Toast being 6 miles from hence we rode to NORWARK where we dined at one John Beldons a very good house & Civil people had a D^r of Lamb roast^d here Sam Burling Joined us & We Set forward in the afternoon for NYork.

Octoe 11th
1750

From Fairfield to NORWALK is 12 Miles here is a pritty river which we Cross And about a mile below the town it is Navigable where We see some small vessels lying but we could not Learn that they had much trade here, from Norwark after dinner we rode to Horse Neck but first called at Stamford which is 10 Miles where we baited at a Sorry house where we had some Sour Madeira wine, 'Tis a tollerable Village and Some good land about it from thence proceeded to Horseneck 6 miles, but before we got there had Exceeding heavy rain was quite dark and Most Intollerable bad road We lodged at one Meads an Illnatur^d old fellow and would Scarce give us lodging tho' we were under the Above hardships & his One Eyed wife little better then himself & wanted a barefooted fellow who we afterwards understood to be her Son to Sleep with one of us but we one & all refused the favour & where he went I Know not neither do I care———

[38]

MADE BY JAMES BIRKET

From that Churlmeads at Horseneck we rode 3 Miles of Most miserable road to Birom river where we Entered the Governm^t of Newyork and presently Found an Alteration in the road & Buildings &C, Everthing from this Bridge bearing the Marks of Industry 7 miles more brought us to Marrowneck where we Breakfasted at a good Clean decent house, and had plenty of Tea Chocolate and Toast And also Sweetmeats, we had not seen Such Cheer since we left Rhode Island And as I observed before Industry appeard in the whole family the Girls hard at work Some Spinning wool others flax &C, from Marrowneck to Kingsbridge is 12 Miles here we dined with Some other Travelers at One Stephensons a Quaker who keeps one of the Best Eating houses we met with, we had a Bass fish taken out of the river by the door before our Eyes & some very good oysters &C This is one of the best built houses for a Tavern I have yet seen in America being all built of good Stone the Apartments large and lofty And a Noble Prospect down towards the Sound; Here we cross the River upon a tall bridge built of wood the Inn & this bridge belong to the Same person; This river is a Branch of the Great North River that breaks out of it a little above this bridge and comes down this way and runs into the Sound above New York and is what makes York Island, & in Spring tides the water flows up this branch until runs Into the North river, but is no at all Navigable As there's abundance of rocks between this bridge and North river, This afternoon

Octoe 12th
1750

Octo 12
1750

SOME CURSORY REMARKS

	we rode from Kingsbridge to New York being 13 Miles of very good road And is near the Length of york Island which is very Narrow but Butified with many handsome Seats belonging to the Gentlemen
Octoe 12th 1750	In york, where we Arriv^d About Sunsett and put up at the Sign of the Horse & Cart in the upper part of the City and prov'd to be very bad lodgings, altho 'tis a house much used
Octoe 13th	Geo: Mifflin and Self dined with Saml Burling, and I went & Lodged with my friend William Coventry——
14	Geo: Mifflin & Self dined wth Wm Coventry & we both went to Meeting——
15	Geo Mifflin Set out for Philadelp^a And I dined with Wm Coventry
16	I dined with John Fell, & Supp^d wth T: Heysham
17	Wm Coventry, David Algeo j^r John Willett Thos Willett & mySelf Cross'd the ferry from NYork to Long Island whereW. C. & mySelf hired a Chais and we all travell^d to Jamaica being 12 Miles where we dined at one Wests, from thince W.Coventry David Algeo jr & Self went to Hempstead plains being 8 Miles And lodged wth D: Algeo Senr
18	We dined at David Algeo's Drank Tea at Gov^e Martins and lodged at David Algeo Senr
19	went to See Parson Davidsons farm, dined at Gov^e Martins, Return^d to Jamaica & Lodged at Wests (8 miles——
Octoe 20 1750	Jamaica is a pretty village and Stands in a Noble plain that Extends for many miles here is a Goal, a Court house, An Episcopal Church, a Dutch

MADE BY JAMES BIRKET

Church, & a presbyterian Meeting house which makes a very pretty Appearance at Some distance having all of handsome little Spires &C We returnd from Jamaica by way of Flatbush a pretty village 10 Miles from Jamaica and 3 from the ferry here is arising ground where I went up and had an Extensive prospect to Sandyhook the Neversinks and out to Sea as also to the Inland part of the Country we got well over the ferry & home to dinner

    At. W: Coventrys rain^d all ye day   Octoe 21st
at My lodgings 23^d at D^o————   22d
Dined at Thomas Heyshams   24
Dined with Isaac Latouch   25
Dined wth John Willett & at James Burlings in   26
the Evening
Dined at John Fells wth H^y Holland   27

        1750
At meetg & Dined wth Sam Burling   Octo 28
Dined with Wm Coventry and in the Afternoon   Do 29
rode out to Harlem and Several other Country Seats in the Neighborhood along with John Fell Samuel Burling Giles Heysham & bought my roan Horse from one Edwd Croston a Butcher who came from Liverpoole which cost me £20

THE PROVINCE OF NEW YORK was first discovered by one Hudson in 1608 And Sold to the Dutch who called it Nova Belgia, But Exception was made agst the Sale by King James as being wthout his Licence, However it remaind in the Hands of the Dutch until the Reign of King Charles the Second when it was taken by Carr and — Nicholls in the

SOME CURSORY REMARKS

year 1664 & Settled by the English, About half the Dutch familys rather then remove themselves Choose to take the Oaths of Fidelity to the King of England and remain in their Settlements, the Descendants of which are Still very Numerous in the Province And very Industrous People——

₁₇₅₀
_{Octoe 29th}

The first bounds of this Province extended as far as Maryland S⁰., the Main Continent as far as they could go the the Westward And Connciticut or a part of New England to the E.ward It is now reduced to a much Narrower Compass, for King Charles 2ᵈ gave all that tract of Land between the North river & Maryland to the Duke of york, the Duke made a Grant of Part of it under Propriaton who called it East & West Jersey which are now the limits of this Province to the Westward, the Likewise Include Long Island (by the Dutch Called —Nassau Island) Statten Island And indeed they Claim all the Islands Eastward as far as Nantucket, but they have only the Name for it Seldom happens that they can get any taxes from them

THE CITY OF NEW YORK (formerly New Amsterdam) is Scituated on the South So : W point of york Island One part of the Town lying upon the

₁₇₅₀
_{Octoe 29th}

Sound that Separates this Island and the Mainland from Long Island, which is the Side of the town where all the Wharfs are Built and the Ships lye, The great North river Washes the other Side of the town faceing the Jerseys which Said river & the Sound Join at the fort at the Lower end of the

MADE BY JAMES BIRKET

town And form a Spacious Bay with many Pretty Small Islands in it

This City is well Scituated for bussiness having the Advantage of all the trade of Connecticut by the Sound as also the coast of Long Island And the Inland Country at least 200 miles by the North river large Sloops go as far as Albany wch is 166 miles and Smaller craft Amongst the Mohawks where they cary on a great trade with the Indians; and, About Albany & Esopus the make the finest flours in America, I was Credibly Inform^d that at the last mention^d place there has been Sold Farms at £50 pAcre taking in the whole Est PMeasure Sandy Hook is reckon'd 10 leagus from the Town this is where we enter the Ocean but I cannot think it so much as we run it down to the Hook in 2 hours indeed we had the Advantage of Wind & tide

Octoe 29
1750

The vessels by this means in the winter are Soon into the Harbour, And Soon out when the wind Serves, when in other ports they are frequently frose up

As I said before the wharfs & places where there vessels lye are on the Eastside of the Town & for the whole Length of it there is a good depth of water And all vessels Load & Discharge without the help of boats or lighters which is very convenient,

Neither their Streets nor houses are at all Regular Some being 4 or 5 Story high & Others not above two, Not any of the Modern houses are built wth the Gable End to the Street as was formerly the fashion amongst all the old Dutch Settlers, but are

1750
Octoe 29

SOME CURSORY REMARKS

many of 'em Spacious Genteel houses Some are built of hewn stone Others of English & Also of the Small white Hollands Brick, which looks neat but not grand, their houses are Generally neat within and well Furnished, Notwithstanding there Still remains too many of the Old Dutch houses which prevents its Appearing to Advantage, The Streets (as above) are very Irregular & Crooked & many of 'em much too Narrow they are Generally pretty well paved which adds much to the decency & Clean-ness of the place & the Advantage of Carriage, The Water in the Pumps & Springs here is a little of the Brackish tast They fetch the Water all without the Gate that they use for Tea &C & several people get their Living by carting of it into town where they Sell it by the pale &C^a

Octoe 29th 1750

Their Publick Buildings are; first the City Hall a large Strong Stone Building the lower part is Seemingly intended for a Change to meet in, as it Stands all upon Arches and is Open like a Market house; Above Stairs are Apartm^{ts} for the Gov^e Councell & Assembly to meet in, And make Laws for the good of the province, there Also is Other Rooms for the Courts of Justice to Sit in, and Order these Laws to be put in due force & Execution And in Order to make the Most of this Building they Have converted the Garratts into a prison for D^{rs} & fellons a Comfortable place Say, take it throughout; the Gov^{e}shouse is in fort George and makes a Good apearance at a distance there was a Church of England Chapell within this fort but was burnt

MADE BY JAMES BIRKET

down in the time of their Negro plot, This fort is well Scituated to maul the Ships as they come up being very low, And close by it to the East ward is a fine battery which mounts a great Number of Guns almost Even with the water's edge; There is also five Market houses fixed at proper distances from the water Side & from One Another, Only three of them is much frequented, And I am of Opinion if they were all Fixed in one place it would be much the best; Here are two Episcopal Churches, which are Large & Strong Buildings of Hewn Stone, and as it must be Allow^d to be the most fashionable religion, So it Seems to me here as well as in most other parts of North America to Prevail here is also Four Dutch Churches Two of the Lutheran the Other of the Calvinistical Order, All which are Large, & formerly were very much crowded but many of the young People fall of to the National form; As do the young people in General from the French Church which now has but a Small Congregation, Here is also A Presbyterian Meeting house which is Large, and has great number of that Society which frequents the Same, and duly attend their prayers, Lectures &C 3 times every Sabath day; One Jews Synagogue, And one meeting of Friends which is but small their Meetinghouse is of Brick which is neat, built about Two years ago, 1 Moravian & 1 Whitfield m^g d^o but both in private houses

The People here are very gay in their dress but more perticularly in the furniture of their houses &C They have of Late a very Extensive trade to

1750
Octo 29

Octoe 29
1750

[45]

SOME CURSORY REMARKS

the Bay of Honduras for Log wood which has been of great Service to the Place in making their Europian Remittances for dry goods &C^a which without this trade puzles them a good deal when bills are Scarce

1750 Octe 29th

They have also An Extensive trade to the Westindies &C^a As, Jamaica St Thomas, Santa Cruz, Surrinam, Curiacoa, in A perticular manner, As Also in a lesser degree to Antigua Barbados, St Kitts &C^a For Bread, Flour, Pork, Beefe, Horses, Lumber, of Sundry sorts as Boards, Plank, Joists, Staves & Heading, Shingles Hoops, & Ranging Timber

They also Build many vessels here of all Sizes, And are well Supply'd with Timber from the Jerseys from Long Island And also from Statten Island which I believe to be the Best in this part of the Country as it grows near the Sea and upon a Clay Soil

1750 Octoe 29th

I would likewise observe that the Trade of the Jerseys is pretty much divided between, New York and Philadelphia, the which is a great Advantage to Both; The Yorkers draw a Great quantity of Bread Flour, and wheat, yearly from the Jerseys by way of Amboy, and down Rariton river by way of Brunswick there being a very good Corn Cuntry up that river

This City also reaps great Advantages by the Navigation of the North or Hudsons river, As the City of Albany lyes so Near the Indians that it

[46]

MADE BY JAMES BIRKET

Enables them to Cary on the furr Trade to greater Advantage then Any other Province in America, And helps them in their Remittances to England

About Ten o'Clock this day I left New York And took the ferry boat for Staten Island Commonly caled Combe's Ferry we were Becalmed upon the water And Expected to've been driven back to N : Y by the floodtide however we got over very well About one o'Clock and went to Vantiles's Tavern being Reckon'd 9 Miles from N York We dined upon Oisters Roasted & Raw and had some Good Madeira Octoe 30

From Vantiles to Elizabeth town point is 6 miles we crossed the Sound here that Seperates Staten Island from the Main Land of the Jerseys into which enter by Crossing this ferry 3 miles further brought us to the Burrough of Eliz^a town, This is a good inland town, but no manner of Regularity in the Streets or houses being built in the Nature of a Good large Village with Some tollerable good houses, They have a Mayor Alderman Recorder &C: Councel from this Town to Woodbridge is 12 Miles this is a good large Country Town and Built Irregularly Much like Elizabeth Town, 3 Miles further brought me to the Antient City of Amboy (als) Perth Amboy I Lodged at the Widdow Serjeants which is the best if not the Only Tavern in the place, This day being the Kings birthday About a dozen Gentlemen met at my lodgings to Spend the Evening to wit, John Richard & Campbell Stevens Dr Johnson John Minikey, John McKivers Andrew Octoe 30th
1750

Octoe 30th
1750

[47]

SOME CURSORY REMARKS

Smyth &C^a we Spent the Evening very agreeably only Sat up a little too late

They have here a Mayor, Alderman, Recorder And Common councel men for the order & Regulation of the City

The Gov^e Councell & Assembly of the Jerseys Meet here and at Burlington Alternately, They have here a Courthouse, a Goal, An Episcopal Church A Presbyterian Meeting house & And a pretty market house but believe but little use for it; I do imagine the Plan of this City has been laid out very regular by the Appearance of Some part of it but being So thin Built and the houses and Gardens &C So interspersst that its hard for a Stranger to form a Notion how the Streets ought to run, however the Houses that are Built are tollerable good and I imagine about 70 or 80 in Number

Octoe 30
1750

This City is built upon a Neck of land that lyes between Rariton river and the Sound that Parts Statten Island from this place; here is a fine Harbour And water enough Up to the Bank Side, Wharfs may be here built with great care and very little Charge, this Place is finely Scituate for trade, as it is so near the Sea, Water Enough at all times to come up to the town, The Sound on one Side of the town and Rariton river on the Other which is Navigable 12 Miles up to the City of Brunswick; Yet by the want of People of Fortune and Spirit to carry on trade the Place is poor And I am of Opinion will remain So as they are Remarkable for their Laziness & the Oppulent City of NYork so near

MADE BY JAMES BIRKET

them that the greatest part of the trade centers there, The People of this City now and then Send a vessel to the west Indies And to Lisbon or Madeira wth wheat but not often, They also build vessels here for wch I think tis an Extraordinary good Scituation, for they have plenty of Timber near them not only in the Jerseys, but also on Staten Island & I take the wood hereabouts to be as good or Better than Any thats farther up the Country as its near the Sea Winds, and upon a Clay Soil And farther A great privaledge or Benefit is that they may thoroughly Soak the plank and timbers in the Sea water *Octo 30th 1750*

The Soil here Seems to Me to be but very poor further inland is much better for Grass or Grain

This morning Set out for Brunswick which is 12 Miles and Stands upon the River Rariton which Cross^d at the Ferry And dined there, Called to See Doctor Messer who lives here and very well, This City is Small, but pretty well built, They have Small craft that comes up here with the flood tide but the river other ways is fordable and a great many banks and Shoals in it, They build Some Sloops and Small vessels here from Brunswick I went to a Small Village Called Kingston 15 Miles & from thence to Prince Town 3 Miles Where I lodged at one Sam: Horners at the Union Flag, A very good Country House and Good Accomoda^{ns} From this little Country Town you Have A noble Prospect (as any I met with in America) towars Egg Harb^r Burlington & Trenton Also to the Northward along way up *31st*

SOME CURSORY REMARKS

1750 Octoe 31st — Rariton river And in the whole over a large Extent of land

Novr 1st — Set forward this Morning and by 10 o'Clock reached Trenton being 12 Miles (Rained all the way) And breakfasted at Elisha Bonds who came from Near Lancaster (I think from Cockram) And his wife from Warrington, as it rain'd I staid and dined here this is a Pretty Small Town that lyes About a Mile from the river Delaware where we cross it at the ferry Called Trenton ferry this is the Extent of the Navigation of the river Above which we See many Rocks above water So that tis Imposible for a Boat to Pass them After dinner I crossed Trenton ferry Entered Pensilvania and Travell'd thro the Mannor of Pensburry which is mostly in woods to Bristol City which is 20 Miles where I Lodged at a tolerable house, Not near so good as Elisha Bonds my Countryman

2d — Set forward this Morning at 8 o'Clock To Neshamony ferry 3 miles to – Frankford a Small village 12 Miles To Philadelphia 5 Miles was there by twelve o'Clock or I believe half an Hour Sooner,

1750 Novr 2d — dined at John Biddles at the Sign of the Indian King in Market Street, from whence in the afternoon I proceeded to Ben Bagnalls in front Street with my fr'd Geo Mifflin where I took Lodgings

3d — I dined with Geo: Mifflin Senr

4 — Dined at home 5 D^o 6th at J^{no} Bringhams

7 — At home Rode in the Afternoon wthG : M And B : B to see Robt Hopkin's Grass
At Point No point

MADE BY JAMES BIRKET

At home Sent Yorkshire wth the 2 horses to R. Hopkins to Grass — 8

At home & Walked in the afternoon to Colthouse's ferry on Schuykill being two miles — 9th

At home 11th at home — 10th

Dined at I: Pemberton jrs 13th at home — 12

At home took a Purge 15th at D^o^ not well — 14

Dined with John Meas. 17th at home — 16

At home. 19th at D^o^ 20th Dined wth Jno Reynells — 18

Dined with John Smith — 21

Dined with Willm Logan 23^d^ At home — 22

At home 25th at D^o^ 26th at D^o^ — 24

At home 28th at D^o^ Much Rain — 27

At home 30th at D^o^ — 29

At home 2^d^ at D^o^ 3^d^ at D^o^— — Decr 1st

Dined with Isaac Greenleafe — 4th

At home 6th at D^o^ 7th at D^o^ — 1750 Decr 5th

At home 9th at D^o^ 10th at D^o^ and I Ordered my roan horse from Grass & Sent him to Stable at the Indian Queen — 8

I Borrow^d^ Ia Pembertons horse and I went wth Israel Pemberton jr to the funeral of Reginere Tyson at Abington being 12 miles Thence to Dunk's ferry upon Delaware 14 Miles which we Cross^d^ And Rode to Burlington wch is 3 Miles Lodged wth Charles Read — 11

we Breakfasted wth Cha. Read and dined with Ebenezar Large where also dined Mary Weston fro London Marg^t^ Bound from New York & Peter Fearon With Sundry others — 12

Burlington is the Chief City or metropolis of

[51]

SOME CURSORY REMARKS

1750 Decr 12th	West Jersey And is Scituate upon the river Delaware Consisting of one Spacious large Street that runs down to the river which makes a fine prospect into Pensilvania with Several Short cross Streets that Terminate in this Principal one, here are tollerable good Buildings And the Land and Country about it very good and Level the Abound wth fine Orchards and Gardens, &C^a They have a good Trade here in Pickled porke And Hams which the Send to the city of Philadelphia for Exportation to the West Indies, Publick buildings are A court house for the Councell And Assembly, underneath which is a Goal this Edifice looks old & makes but a Poor figure Considering the Advantageous Scituation being built in this fine Open street there is Also An Episcopal Church and two friends Meeting houses
	This Afternoon Return^d back over Dunk's ferry to Philadelphia wch is 20 Miles in Comp^a wth s^d M Weston Margaret Bownd Saml Bowne Is: Greenleafe I: Pemberton jr &C^a ———
13	Dined at John Mifflins and walk^d in the Afternoon to Schuykill
14	At home went in the Afternoon over the ferry to the Jerseys in comp^a wth G Mifflin jr & B: Bagnall And returned in the Evening
15	At home 16th at home Hard frost
17	At home 18th at D^o writing letters frosty
19	At home 20 at D^o 21st at home Rain, Snow, And violent wind
1750 Decr 22d	At home all day, Snow, D^o Sent P Bard to

MADE BY JAMES BIRKET

Antigua 2 half bushels, bees wax, 2 Rounds beefe And 3 hats——

At home Drink't tea wth Jno Reynells	23d
At home a Pleasant day 25thDined with Thomas Hatton & Capt Phillips	24
At home Rained all day	26
At home and hard frost	27
At home Hard frost and very Cold	28
At home Hard frost, the Ice So strong as to bear over the river, The Coldest day that has been for many years	29
At home	30
Set out for Mary Land in Company with Mary Weston, Easter White, Ia: Pemberton Israel Pemberton jr Wm Logan And Sundry others to the lower ferry on Schuylkill is 3 miles thence to Darby 5 miles And to Chester 8 miles where we dined at the Widdow Lloyds this town Stands upon the riv^e Delaware And one Might Imagine well Scituate for trade but I could not Perceive the least traces of any thing of the kind it is the Metropolis of the County and has courts of Judicature held there I do not See its Remarkable for any thing Else; from Chester to Brandy Wine toll Bridge 14 Miles to Wilmington 3 Miles we lodged at One Ganthonys This Town is a very modern one being but a few years Since it was first laid out & built all the houses being new & built of Brick, is in a very good country for Wheat and flour, Abundance of which is brought here for Sale the Greatest part of which is sent up to Philad^a in Shallops, and a part Shipt by	31st 1750 Decr 31st

[53]

SOME CURSORY REMARKS

the Inhabitants for the Westindies but the Inhabitants being many of them in low Circumstances cannot make any great figure in trade this town lyes about 2 or 3 miles from the River Delaware on a Creek Called Christeen Creek but have water enough for good vessels up to their Wharfs where they may load or discharge

Jane 1st   This Morning we set out and got to Ogletown 12 Miles (Near this place we Enter Cecil County in Maryland) where we dined, from thence to the Head of Elke river 9 Miles, Thence by the head of North East And Principio Iron works to Susquehannah ferry is 15 Miles, where we lodged at the ferry house & Good Entertainm^t

1750-1
Jane 2d   This morning we passed the Great river Susquehannah upon the Ice, the river here is deem^d 3 miles over, the horses were led over before us and we followed on foot only the two women had each a Ladder laid down upon the Ice and there baggage thereon, upon wch they Sat down and were drawn over by 2 Men; who Slipt of their shoes and run so fast that we could not keep way with them, This ferry is Just at the head of Chesapeak bay, from whence we Proceeded to Jacob Giles's in Baltimore County 3 Miles where we dined, And in the Afternoon we went to Wm Coxes at Rock run Thro' large tall woods all the way (Except Some very small Plantations being 6 miles where we Lodged

3d   From Wm Coxes we went to dear creek to A Meet^g and Called by the way at An Iron forge

MADE BY JAMES BIRKET

which is large and Extreemly well fitted, they work three fires which are at a good distance from One Another, and the roofe being raised very high, they must be well adapted for that hot Country in the Summer Season here the work 2 hammers one for the Chaffry and one for the Two finerys one of wch is Blown by a pair of wooden Bellows that are fixed with Springs within but I cannot describe the Nature of the working, with Pen and Ink, only the may be Observed they are of the Same Shape and the Bellow boards and Harness the Same to a trifle as those done with Leather —— from Coxe's to dearcreek is 5 miles we dined at our friend James Rigbys and in the afternoon travell^d through the woods to James Lees is 5 miles where we lodged

1751
Jane 3d

This Morning we rode from Ja^s Lees to Bush river meetg 12 Miles, Thro'. Wood, and very uneaven Ground, hard frost & Snow upon the Ground, The woods here Abouts are the Tallest I see any where in North America, And I believe the Soil is very good but very little of it Cleared; here I met Stephen Onion Esqr who I had Corosponded wth Several years, And went with him to his house 9 Miles to Gun powder Ironworks where I lodged, he lives very Genteely And has Close by his house 2 Iron forges An Iron Furnace a Grist mill and A Large Smiths Shop where all Kinds of Black work is done And a Saw Mill for Boards or any other Kind of Timber for the use of his works, he has here plenty of water and a Good head and his dam is very large and at the Same time not above

4th

1750
Jane 4th

[55]

SOME CURSORY REMARKS

100 yards from the forge, he has dug a Channel through a Rock that brings the Water out of the upper dam to both forges and the furnace is ab^t 200 yards below the forges his Iron mines are Just by his works, and for wood it Abounds in this County as I observed before, very little Clear'd ground to be met with, I here See a pair of wooden Bellows open and had an Opertunity to view them more Satisfactorily then those wch were at work at Dear Creek forge the Shell or rim of the upper bellowboard Slides over the lower one, as the upper part of a Box goes down upon the Bottom part and there is a great number of Short Square peices of Wood which are Should^{ed} one upon Another and kept close together with Springs to prevent the Air's Escaping between the upper And lower part that Slides over each other.

upper And lower part that Slides over each other.

1751
Jane 5th

This day came from Isaac Websters Several of our Company & Dined at Stephen Onions, after which MW E.W. John Giles &C Set out for the river of Potomack and Virginia & about 4 o'Clock and hard frost I. P. And Self set our for Jacob Giles's by way of Joppa to Bush river land^g 8 Miles where there is a very good furnace, but being dark we had not an Opportunity of viewing the Same we baited here and then rode to Jacob Giles's 12 Miles where got about 9 at night and was very kindly rece^d I observe in all this County the Country is mighty uneven, And quick rising & falling, in the road, and the Country all Cloathed with tall timber

MADE BY JAMES BIRKET

trees of different Species, the largest & talest kind I observed the call a tulep tree, bark^d very much like an oak but Something of a dead flower remains upon the Branches all the Winter, which in Some sort resembles a tulep, And Appears at A distance to be a flower in full bloom this wood makes good boards for the Inside work of a house being very white and free from knots, but at the Same time very Soft and Spungy

here are few plantations Clear'd & those very small There houses in General very bad and ill contrived there furniture mean; there Cooks and houswifry worse if possible Except at S: O. And J: G. where we were Genteely Entertaind both as to Eating, drinking, And Lodging

I. Pemberton & Self Set out this Morning for Philadelphia (hard frost and has been all this week) and came to Susquehannah river 3 miles where crossed the Same upon the Ice which is called 3 Miles More, hence to Principio Ironworks is 5 Miles, These were the first works in the Country as the name denotes, hence to North East Iron Works is 2 Miles where we called and baited with the Chiefe Manager, One Baxter who is in the Commission of the Peace, and has the direction of these & Principio works they belong to a Company in Londⁿ and are Esteem^d to make the best Iron And they Certainly have the best workmen in America but I observe they all Employ many negros in their works, these works as will as those on the other side of Susquehannah are very large and comodiūs;

1750-1
Jane 5th

Jane 6th

SOME CURSORY REMARKS

hence to the Head of Elk river 8 miles to Ogletown 9 miles dined at Ogles the propr^r who keeps a tollerable good tavern, the Ground here begins to be more generally Clear'd, and Appears to be pretty good, Hence to Wilmington is 12 Miles Lodged wth David Farris had our horses at Jos: Littlers, And Snow'd all the way from 'Squ^e Baxters

Jan^e 7   Staid at Willmington, Snowed all the day, Went to See B: Shipley & my old Acquaintance Ro^t Richardson Israel Pemberton left me ye morn'g & rode home—

Jan^e 8th   Set forward (deep Snow) from hence to Brandywine Tolbridge 3 Miles to Chester 14 Miles where I

1750-1
Jan^e 8th   dined at a very good house And had Some Mull^d Cyder to Keep up our Spirits, very Cold, from Chester I got next to Schuylkill ferry (by way of Darby a very good village in the way) 13 miles thence to the City of Philadelphia 3 Miles and got to my lodgings before dark

Do 9th   At home 10 at home 11 At home

12   Ben Bagnall & Wife T: Bagnell *Geo Mifflin* John Lacy P. Newbury and my Self went in two Slays to Germin Town being 6 miles to dinner and returned in the Even.g in 40 Minutes this kind of traveling is only whilst the Snow continues upon the Ground, as they have no wheels but only Stands upon two pieces of wood that Lyes flat on the Ground like a North of England Sled, the fore part turning up with a bent to Slyde over Stones or any little rising and are Shod with Smooth Plates of Iron to prevent their wearing Away too fast. . . .

MADE BY JAMES BIRKET

The Sides of this Machine are boarded up about 18 Inches high & the Ends Much higher with one seat forward and the other behind, each holds two persons compleat as a Coach the 2 horses are Harness^d in the same manner as for a Wheel carriage abating for the goodness, and a pole from the forepart lyes between the horses as in a Charrot, the driver Stands right up in the forepart of the Slay and goes at a prodigeous Speed, All Ranks of people Covet this kind of Traveling or divertion for whilst the Snow lyes upon the ground all the Carters or dray men lay all other business aside And Stand as regularly at proper places to be hired (as the Hackney Coaches do in London) to go to the Neighbouring villages there to Eat, drink & return in the Eveng & Some later enough at Night

At home begun to thaw very fast and rain^d all day, and towards Eveng the Ice in the River begun to break

1751
Jane 12th

13th

At home 15th at D^o 16th at D^o rainy Weather
17th I dined at John Mifflins
18 I dined at George Mifflins Senr
At Home 20th at D^o 21st at D^o
At home & We had the Most violent gale of wind at S^o and S&BW which some one Brig. at the Wharfe very much damaged another, And indeed several vessels And houses Suffered greatly, the top of the Wind mill Aposite to the town blown of, And its said there has not been so much damage rece^d here the many years

1750-1
Jane 14th

19th
22d

SOME CURSORY REMARKS

23d At home Spent the evening wth Jos Saunders
24th At home 25th at D^o Walked to Colthouse's
26th At home 27th at D^o 28th at home had a Coat & Breeches made by I. Fullerton

29th I went to the Superior Court held at the State house when there was brought before the Court upon an Indictement for house breaking And Accessorys John Morris Eliz^a Robinson Jno Crow Francis McCoy and his wife And John Stinson, before Chiefe Justice Allen & Judge......... John

1750-1 Jane 29th Morris Pleaded Guilty, McCoy and his Wife Robinson Crow & Stinson Pleaded not Guilty, A lad from Maryland (who followed this Robinson from thence hearing She was in Goal here last year And bound himself Printice to raise some money to procure her freedom, & then She and he with others, was to Steal to raise Money to buy his time out) *one* Turner by name being also taken up one of the first of the Gang & Exam^d turn'd Kings Evidence agst all the rest And was the Most Material witness against them And after a tryall of Near 9 hours the Jury bro^t, in McCoy, Robinson & Crow Guilty Accord^g to the Indictm^t As Accesarys before the fact Commited Stinson Guilty as an Accessary after the fact committed by Consealing Morris in his house w^h Search was made for him by the proper offecers, and a reward of £60 offerd for the Aprehending of him, McCoy's Wife not Guilty, As acting under the Coersive power of her husband

1750-1 Jane 30th I was in Court when Morris Robinson Crow And McCoy rece^d Sentence of death Stinson was brought

MADE BY JAMES BIRKET

in Guilty but he Pleading a Certain Act which is Equall to the Benefit of the Clergy was only burnt in the hand, and that Moderately enough, And orderd to give Security for twelve months And the forfeiture of all his goods and Chattels......

I dined with John Meas	31st
I dined with John Bringhurst	Febyr 1st
At home Wrote to Sundrys P Mitchel at Lond:	2d
At home dined With Jos: Crosby	3d
At home at Q^{ty} Meetg 5th At home &C^a	4th
At home 7th Dined wth Tho Hatton and at Capt T. Phillips in ye Afternoon	6
At home	8.
Dined at home in the Afternoon John Pickering jr & Self went home with Owen Evans Esqr to Northwales being 20 Miles which we Rode in 3^h 25^m	9th
We went to N^{o}Wales Meeting	10
Continued wth O: E being a Stormy day	11
From O: Evans we Called at J: Evans So to German Town And home Owen Evans with us	12
I this day dined wth Is: Pemberton Senr & My old Acquaintance Jonah Thompson And this day were Executed on the Common John Morris, Fr: McCoy & Eliz^a Robinson; John Crow was Reprieved under the Gallows & this Evening Capt John Lacy of Whitby Sailed hence for Virginia	1750-1 Feby 13th
At home & M.g Dined wth Wm Logan	14th
At home Great rain & Snow	15
At home 17 D^o & at M.g	16.
At home Settling Acc^{ts} wth Sundrys	18

SOME CURSORY REMARKS

19.	At home......D⁰......
20.	At home......D⁰......
21.	At home & M.g
22d	At home and in the Evening had a few friends at the Coffee hº
23d	At home & Dined wth Is: Pemberton jr
24	At home And At M.g, And now According to My former Method I shall Proceed to Say Somthing of the Province of Pensilvania & City of Philadelphea before before My Departure for N: York

1750-1
Feby 24th

PENSILVANIA is one of the most considerable of the Northern Colonies William Pen Esqr Son of Sr WmPen obtained the Grant for this Province in 1679 and gave it the Name of Pensilvania by which name it is called in the Original Patent from King Charles the 2d dated the 4th March 1680 And Contains a tract of Land lying between the beginning of the 40th 43d degree of North Latd and bounded by the River Delaware to the East which Separated this Province from NJersey, To the North by the Indian Nations to the west & South by Maryland and the Sea; This Province has Increased more in its Inhabitants then Any of its Neighbours, Owing to the Number of German & Irish Passengers who Anually come here and Settle with their wives & familys often 4 or 5000 in a year Many of which are now become People of extensive fortunes, both in the Towns and likewise in the Country after the first grant of Pensilvania which containd the three uper Counties of Buckingham,

[62]

MADE BY JAMES BIRKET

Philadelphia, and Chester, By King Charles the Second; Pen Obtaind a Another Grant from the Duke of York for part of Nova Belgia or the Province of New York which lyes between Maryland and the River Delaware, from Marcus Hook 4 miles below Chester along the river 120 Miles & terminates 20 Miles below Henopen, this is computed to be 40 Miles deep between the Delaware & Maryland and is divided into the 3 lower Counties Called Newcastle, Kent, & Sussex, Notwithstanding they have but one Gov^e over the whole, yet the three lower counties have their own Separate councel & Assembly, make their own Laws, Their own Paper Currency and hold their own Assemblys at Newcastle, where the Gov^e Attends during their Deliberations, as he does at Philadelphia for the 3 upper Counties 1750-1 Feby 24th

The Gov^e is Apointed by the Propriators And confirmed by the King, their Assembly is Choose Anually and commonly make two Sessions or Sittings (viz') In January & August at Philadelphia I do not Know w^t time the Assembly for the Lower Countys Sit but it must be Some part of the Interval between the Sittings at Philadelphia upon Accot of ye Gov^e being obliged to be there 1750-1 Feby 24th

PHILADELPHIA is the Capital of the Province, and perhaps one of the best Laid out Citys in the world and if built According to the Plan wo^d be large enough for the Head of an Empire it is An Oblong Square Extending betwist two Navigable rivers the Delaware And Schuylkill two miles in

SOME CURSORY REMARKS

        length And the long streets 9 in Number from E^t to W^t between river & River, to be cut at Right Angles by others of one Mile in Length and Twenty in Number fro. N^o to S^o all Straight as a Line & Spacious But as the first Settlers of this City begun upon the Banks of Delaware

1750-1
Feby 24th

For more then a Mile in Length they have not been Able to Build so far Inland between the two Rivers as to Come Near the place intended for the Center of the City, the furthest that is yet Built upon is either 6th or 7th Street from Delaware exclusive of a Certain Street built between Front street and the River called water Street one Side of which is mostly built upon ground made out of the river & was never Intended in the Original Plan of the City which is well Scituated fore Trade Tis about one Hundred & twenty Eight miles from this City to Cape Henlopen or Lewis Town and very good Navigation in General, tis in *most places 6 or 7 fathom in the Stream And to the Wharfs the have water enough for Large Ships to load & unload without the help of boats or lighters, the river here is three quarters of a Mile wide And has Islands in it Above & below the Town

1750-1
Feby 24th

There is belonging to this town a great Number of Ships, and from hence a very Extensive trade is Carr^d on to all the English Islands in the west Indies for Bread, Flour, Porke, Hams, Indian Corn, Buckwheat Oats, Apples &C^a, Also hogshead & Barrel Staves & heading of white Oak Esteem^d the Best in NAmerica, Shingles, Hoops, Bar Iron &C. also live

     * See the End of this Itinerary

MADE BY JAMES BIRKET

Stock as Sheep, Geese, Turkeys, Ducks & fowles in great Plenty; But Some of their Chiefe men and Such as fill the Most Stble places & Posts in the Governm^t drive on a very large & Contraband Trade with the French at Leogan, the cape, &C for Sugar And Molosses, to the great damage of the Honest And fair Trader.

They have also a good trade for wheat, Staves &C^a, to Madeira, Lisbon, And Several parts of Spain, to Say Nothing of that Extensive trade between them & their Mother Country for Black wallnut and other valuable wood of different kinds, Large Q^{tys} of Pig and Bar Iron and that of an Excellent Quality, by Encouragem^t large quantitys of Hemp might be raised here, And as to Flax they raise Abundance it is Supposed that in the Article of Flax-seed Produced in this province the receive from Ireland upwards of 40,000 annually

The Publick buildings in this City are, first the State house which was built in the year 1732 and is Esteem^d a Grand Eddifice for (besides a Lobby in the Center the Dementions of wch is 40 by 20 feet) There are Two rooms of 40 feet Square and 30 feet high (one on Each Side said Lobby) the one for the Assembly, the Other for the Supream Court or Grand sessions on the 2d floor is the Councel Chamber And Committee room, And a Gallery of 100 feet Long, Adjoining to W^{ch} on the South side of the Same is a Large Tower & Cupulo wth a bell in it

This Bell is used during the Sitting of the Assembly to Call them together at the Same hour— Here

1750-1
Feby 24th

1750-1
Feby 24th

SOME CURSORY REMARKS

is also in The Broad or Market street a Guild or Town hall, where the Courts of Common Pleas are held, and also the City Courts & Other Publick bussiness is Transacted And under which is a Market house and upon Other days Publick vendues are Carried on here; Also 2 other Publick market Places upon Society hill; Likewise a very large building errected by Whitfield and his followers but Sold by them and now Converted into An Academy for youth in the different branches of Learning and Succeeds to Admiration, Likewise the Quakers School house, which which is a good pile of Building, The Quakers Alms house, The City alms house, the Infirmary, The Hospital, The Goal And the workhouse; as to Places of Worship there is the Episcopal Church w[ch] is large, and of Late has rece[d] the Addition of a Steeple, and Spire,

1750-1
Feby 24th

There is also 2 Quakers Meetg houses and another Building upon Society hill, 2 Presbiterian meeting houses, One Baptist meeting house, one dutch Calvinist & one dutch Lutheran Church, one Moravian D[o] one Sweeds Church, And one of the Methodist or Whitfieldians which was built by the Charity of the Inhabitants and has the noted Gilbert Tennant for their Pastor; one Romish Chappel, which I believe compleats the Number of Places of worship, Here is in this City Some Jews, but they are not allowed any Place of Public Worship as not being of the Christian Profession

In the year 1749 the Houses in this City were Carefully Number[d] And found to Amount to 2076

MADE BY JAMES BIRKET

By which it Appears to be the Largest City in our America for in the year 1746 by an Exact Acc⁰ And that upon Path, there was only 1760 Dwelling houses in Boston and in New York in the year 1751 there was 2050 houses, By which Accots And Also another that was taken at Philada in the year 1750 there then was in that City 2100 dwelling houses, And the greatest part of them built of Brick and three Storys high, and well Sashed, So that this city must make (take it upon the whole) a very good figure, and only wants the Streets to be Paved to make it appear to advantage, for there is few Towns if any in England that are better Illumind with Lamps & those of the best Sort, nor their watch better regulated,

*This city is Governd by a Mayr Recorder and 24 aldermen Common Councell men And other of inferior Officers as usual

    1750-1
    Feby 24th

I forgot to mention a very good Library that is well Kept in the left wing of the State house, and in wch is a large Collection of Books on Different Subjects which are Lent out by the Library Keeper upon a Note being given by the Borrower to return the Book in a Certain time, and an Acknowledgment to the Propriators for the Use of it— Likewise James Logan Built in his lifetime a Library for the Reception of his valuable collection, but was not Compleated when I was there

German Town Seven Miles from Philadelphia Consists but of one Street and is Chiefly inhabited

* See the latter end of this Itinerary

SOME CURSORY REMARKS

by Germans, 'tis near 2 Miles long & carries on a very great Trade in Making Stockings &C both of thread and Woolen yarn wch is Milled and thereby made very warm And Suitable to their weather Lancaster I am informed is a large and a thriving town Scituate About 60 Miles inLand and the Chiefe part of the Town belongs to the Present Gov^e Ja Hamilton They Produce in that part abundance of Excellent Wheat flax &C &C The Propriators are now Thomas & Richard Pen Esq^{rs} What Improvm^{ts} may in time be made is hardly to be guess^d at, but I was well Informed that the Anual income is Clear £25000 Cash, that Curry, or upwards of £15,000 Sterg̃

1750-1
Feby 24th

Notwithstanding the great Numbers of Germans and others that yearly Arrive and Settle in this Province, yet in many places the ground remains uncultivated & Abundance of wood land remains yet uncleared; Their oak timber in this Governm^t Seems to me to be of the very worse Quality of Any in America, I observe in divers places where very tall fine Oaks to Apearance has been blown down by hard gales of Wind Pticularly in the Mannor of Pensburry, that in a Short time the whole Trunk that laid upon the Ground would Moulder into dirt and So lay upon the Ground in a ridge the whole Length of the tree plainly Shewing where it laid, tho' nothing but a Ridge of Mud or dirt remains So that it is Evident to me that Vessels built in this Country, without Some method of Seasoning the Materiels

MADE BY JAMES BIRKET

very well, both timber & Plank must decay in a very Short time

I will only Observe that Philad^a is Remarkable for having the largest and best Market in America it Abounds with Beefe, Mutton, veal, Porke, all kinds of Poultry as Turkeys wild & tame, Geese, ducks Wild & tame, Dunghill fowls, Pheasants, Quails, wild Pidgeons, also Venison as fallow Deer in abundance, Rabbits, &C And great Plenty of fruite & Roots as Potatoes, Turneps, Parsneps Carratts Cabbage &C &C

1750-1
Feby 25th

This day tooke leave of my friends in Philadelphia, Dined with B Bagnell & about 2 o'Clock Set out for Burlington Ia: Pemberton Tho: Crosby Sam: Burge went with me to Frankfort 5 Miles And George Mifflin & Ben: Bagnall went with me to Burlington we Crossed at Dunk's ferry, To Burlington is 15 Miles fro: Frankfort and all good Road, I need not Say anyting further of Burlington having mention'd it 12th Decr last

26

Lodged last night at the Tavern, this day at Meeting J Thompson from Eng^d there as also Gov^e Belcher And Sundry People of Distinction, Dined wth Charles Read Speaker of the Assembly, and in the afternoon Crossed the ferry here from the City of Burlington to the City of Bristol in Pensilvania Goverm^t As Burlington is in the Jerseys— Bristol has the name of a City but in England would make but a poor village however it is Pleasantly Scituate upon the Bank of the River Delaware from hence

[69]

SOME CURSORY REMARKS

I went this Evening to Trenton (12 Miles) to Elisha Bonds All night

1750-1
Feby 27th
Set out this morning from Trenton in W^tJersey to Prince Town (12 Miles) and Breakfasted with one Sam^e Horner from Thence to Brunswick 18 miles Dined; Cross^d the ferry here and got to Perth Amboy this Evening & Lodg^d at the Widdow Sarjeants, 12 *miles*

28th
Over Amboy ferry this morning to Staten Island (see Acco^t Amboy Octo 30th) and thence Along s^d Island to the Narrows being 18 miles Over the ferry 2 Miles And dined at the ferry house (where I see my Old Acquaintance Ben Bispham Coming from NYork to his own house at Mt Holy in the Jerseys) from this house to the Village of Flat Bush is 5 Miles, from thence to NYork ferry house upon long Island is 5 miles Blowing hard here I staid all night

March 1st
This morning I went over at the ferry to NYork and dined wth Wm Coventry

2d
Lodged wth Wm Coventry & Dined wth D^o

3d
At Meeting dined & Supp^d wthM Bowne

4
Dined wth Isaac Latouch
D^o Supp^d wth John Axell (W C. there)

5
Dined wth Thos Duncan in wall Street
Snow Yesterday & this day

1750-1
March 6th
I dined wth William Coventry

7.
I dined with John Willett Esqr

8.
I set out over the ferry Called at Ramseys at the ferry house for my horse where I left him when I

MADE BY JAMES BIRKET

returned to NYork from hence to Jamaica 12 Miles & Called at Wests an Excellent house where I baited & proceeded to David Allgeo's upon Hampstead plains (8 miles) drank tea at Coll⁰ Martins at David Allgeo's All night

Came from David Allgeo's to Jamaica '8 Baited at Wests to new York in the Evening 12 Miles Left my horse at the ferry house Kept by Ramsey   9th

At meeting at NYork dined wth Ia Burling Supped with D⁰———   10

   Dined wth Saml Burling Supp^d wth Wm Coventry.   11.
   Dined wth W. C 13th Dined wth D⁰ Coventrys   12
   Dined wth Capt Ralph Hilton   14
   Dined wth Wm Coventry   15
   This morning took leave of my friends in N York (viz) Wm Coventry Is: Latouch Jos. Haynes Nat. Marsten Ra Hilton Tho: Duncan, Ia Burling, Sam Burling John Fell &C &C^a Had a Bowl of Hot Arrack and went Imediately aboard the Snow Elizabeth Giles Heysham   16.

On Board the Eliz^a Giles Heysham Mas^r for Antigua wth John Willett Esqr Chas Duncan And my Self Passengers Also Yorkshire & the Two Horses, Wind N W And a fine gale We turn^d off our fast from the Wharfe at 10 o'Clock A.M. and at One o'Clock we Passed by Sandy hook   1750-1 March 16th

   Fine day Wind N W Course S E   .17
   D⁰ & fresh gale @ D⁰————D⁰   18.
   D⁰ & D⁰.... @ D⁰————D⁰   19.
   Hard gale @ S:W————D⁰   20

SOME CURSORY REMARKS

21	Exceeding fine Weather wind N W———D⁰
22	D⁰— wind @ S W........D⁰
23	D⁰ Wind N W–Lat 31° 46'———D⁰
.24	Fresh Gale W^d W^terly wth Thunde &C Lat^d 29° 56' Antigua this day bears S⁰ B W 783'
1751., 25	Fresh Gale @ S W & N W Lat 27°,,26'
26	Wind Westerly and Near Noon begun to dye away Lat 26°,,26'. Near Calm the Afternoon and the follow^g night
27.	At 8 this Morn^g the Breese came About to the N E. See a Sloop to the East^wd the latter part of this day had a fine Trade at N E Lat: POb: 25°,,55'.
28	A fine Trade E N E. POb: 23°,,41'
29.	D⁰————D⁰—Pob 22°1'
30	D⁰———— ——— — 20°,,9'
.31	D⁰—and Pleasant gale Pob: 18°,,10'
1751 Apl 1	Smart gail at E B S and ES E Lat: 16° 30' at noon begun to Steer W. B. S. & See Sev^e men War birds And See a vessel in the Morn^g from the Masthead
2d	Fine Weather Steer^d W½N. Lat POb 16°,,42' in the Even^g Caught a booby on the try Sail gaff
3d	Between 3 and 5 this morn^g laid to, very Squally at ¾ past 10 o'Clock made the Island Antigua Dist: about 6 Leagues at one was off willoughby bay and at 6 got up wth Sandy Island Tacked and came too under Hawksbill all night where we laid very Safely———

MADE BY JAMES BIRKET

Got under Sail at 6 o'Clock this morng and turned into St John's Harbour got Ashore at 10 AM, In good health and Thanks be to God found all my friends well After a voyage of 8mo^s & 9 days from this Island I travelled in this Journey upon the Continent of N. America about 1120 miles—

Boston .... N. B. in page [22] See an Acco^t of the Long Wharf there, to which I add that our fr'd Jabez Maud Fisher of Philadelphia when here vizt 24th of Octo^r 1775 told me that he had Measured the Long Wharfe at Boston & found it 700 yards long which is less than Reported by 180 yards........

Philadelphia .... See page [64] There was 2 Friends Meeting Houses & another Building on Society hill Said Fisher above told me there is now Four Meeting houses belonging to Friends wch Consist of 800 Families & which are Reckoned at 2700 Individuals.......

Ditto .. .. Also that the Tide of flood rises only 6 feet at that City being 128 miles from Cape Henlopen near Lewes Town Also

Ditto.. .... as the Streets are Intersected at right Angles makes Intermediate Squares – 450 feet or 150 yards Fronting each way

SOME CURSORY REMARKS

I had Recommendations to the following Gentlemen at Boston by sundry persons
Andrew Mackonzie—By Sam: Horner—
Benj^a Faneuil.... By D^o..........
Capt W^{m}Morris ....By D^o..........
Foster Hutchinson Did Business wth him
A Letter from Capt Edwd Cahill for John Erving..
D^o......D^o.... for Thos Hubard
D^o......D^o....James Forbes..
D^o one for Henry Oassals Esqr my true fr'd—
D^o one for John Fenton ....
D^o one for Thomas Goodthwaite ......